Pronghorn on the Powder River

BY BERNIECE FRESCHET

Illustrated by Robert Quackenbush

On the high Montana plains a herd of pronghorn antelope ranges today, as their ancestors did millions of years ago. Around and above them circle their enemies — coyote and cougar, eagle and bobcat. For these wild beautiful creatures of the plains, life is always harsh, but no other animal is as swift in eluding pursuit. Others may run for thicket or forest, but the pronghorn stays in the open, always outrunning his foe.

The life of the pronghorn is vividly portrayed here by a skillful nature writer whose knowledge and affection for the rugged Western country and its creatures is strikingly matched by Robert Quackenbush's dramatic illustrations.

Pronghorn on the Powder River

Pronghorn on the Powder River

BY BERNIECE FRESCHET

Illustrated by ROBERT QUACKENBUSH

THOMAS Y. CROWELL COMPANY/New York

BY THE AUTHOR

Beaver on the Sawtooth

The Jumping Mouse

Pronghorn on the Powder River

Skunk Baby

Designed by Carole Fern Halpert
Manufactured in the United States of America

Library of Congress Cataloging in Publication Data
Freschet, Berniece.
  Pronghorn on the Powder River.
  SUMMARY: During his first year of life on the Great Plains, a pronghorn learns from his
mother the techniques of survival.
  1. Pronghorn antelope—Juv. lit.
[1. Pronghorn antelope] I. Quackenbush, Robert M., illus. II. Title.
QL737.U52F73   599′.7358   72–12835
ISBN 0-690-65886-9
ISBN 0-690-65887-7 (lib. bdg.)

1   2   3   4   5   6   7   8   9   10

In memory of my father Paul Speck, who homesteaded on the Powder River, and for my brothers Paul and Vernon, who were born in the log house my father built there.

It was a sunny May morning.

Cloud shadows drifted across the high Montana plains while from a lone cottonwood tree a yellow-breasted meadowlark tilted his head and sang a spring song.

As far as the eye could see, new shoots of green grass rippled in the soft breeze.

On a knoll outlined against the blue sky, a herd of pronghorn antelope grazed—animals found nowhere in the world except in America.

The pronghorn's ancestors lived on the North American continent between one and two million years ago, and today's pronghorn looks almost the same as his ancestors of long ago.

Hunters of the Old West called him goat or antelope, but he is neither antelope nor goat nor deer. Although he has the characteristics of several animals, he is the only animal in his family—the *Antilocapridae.*

These creatures are the hunted.

Above and all about them are shadowy pursuers that they must constantly guard against—the meat eaters—coyote and cougar, eagle and bobcat. It has always been so.

On these plains many animals depend on speed to escape their enemies, but none is so swift as the American pronghorn. Other animals may run for thicket and forest in which to hide, but the pronghorn always stays in the open, outrunning his pursuers.

Suddenly alert, the herd lifted proud heads and looked out over the Great Plains. The restless animals flicked their tails.

A young doe edged nervously away from the herd and trotted off between the gray-green shrubs of sage. At the top of a rise she paused to look back. For a moment she stood, her head high, a beautiful wild creature of the plains.

Sunshine glistened on her coat. The hair on her back and sides was a tan and russet color, while that along her neck was tipped with black. Her chest and undersides were white, as was the round patch across her rump.

Her hoofs and horns were shiny black. She had long pointed ears, and two crescent bands of white circled her throat, framing her handsome head.

She darted down the rolling slope.

A sage hen scurried into the brush.

In a short while the herd was out of sight. All around her the land was filled with the sounds and color of springtime. Clusters of purple and white clover blossomed on the prairie; in a sudden whirr of wings, over a hundred blackbirds rose quickly into the air, singing together.

The young doe continued on her way, intent on finding a spot that was hidden and shady. She moved into a shallow gully thick with bushes of choke cherry. She had found the place she was looking for.

Hidden in the choke cherry thicket, on a soft grassy bed, the young doe's fawns were born—twin sons. Carefully, she licked and nuzzled her little fawns.

They were beautifully marked with coats of reddish brown and underpatches of white. Their colors blended with the background, making them invisible to prowling enemies. They had almost no odor—nature's way to protect these helpless creatures.

Although they weighed only four pounds apiece, in minutes after their birth, Lightfoot and Flagtail were struggling to get up. In a short while they stood, on long, sticklike legs. Wobbling uncertainly, they took a few stumbling steps.

Almost immediately the mother doe hid her newborn fawns in separate places a hundred yards apart. If an enemy found one of them, the other might go unnoticed. She taught them to remain very still.

The doe grazed a short distance away from her young and never went near them except at feeding time. She kept a sharp lookout for enemies and jealously guarded her fawns.

Lightfoot and Flagtail learned to flatten their bodies close against the dirt, hugging the ground. The coloring of their coats made them look like small mounds of earth. They kept very quiet until their mother came and nudged them to stand.

Even the sharp eyes of the eagle overhead could not find the baby fawns.

One dusky evening, when Lightfoot was almost a week old, he lay quietly waiting for his mother to come and nurse him. The doe was late and Lightfoot was hungry. He gave a squeaky bleat, expecting her to come at once. He waited but she did not come.

Cautiously, he lifted his head. He could see only bushy stems of the sagebrush. His mother was nowhere in sight. He waited a while longer, but hunger finally prodded him to his feet. He looked around. He saw his mother bound over the top of a ridge and sprint toward him. The gray shadow of a coyote raced after her.

It was too late for the doe to try and lure the enemy away from her fawns—the coyote had seen Lightfoot. Now the doe had to turn and fight if she was to save her young.

At the hiding place she faced her pursuer. Lightfoot reacted quickly to his mother's signal of danger and jumped under her body.

Loping easily, the coyote came steadily toward them. Ten feet away he halted.

Lightfoot looked out from between his mother's forelegs. He saw the coyote's yellow eyes flash and heard a low growl—he saw the sharp, pointed teeth.

The enemy crept closer.

Suddenly his mother bounded forward! She leaped into the air and slashed downward with her strong hoofs.

Lightfoot watched his mother attack, his small body trembling with fear.

She jumped quickly, spinning first one way and then another—always facing her enemy. Again and again the furious doe leaped, striking down with her sharp front hoofs—always keeping herself between the coyote and her fawn.

Finally, bruised and bleeding, the coyote gave up the battle. Now his one aim was to escape the determined attack of the angry doe. He ran—his tail low to the ground.

Lightfoot's mother came and nuzzled him to be sure he was unhurt. She licked his face. Her warm tongue and gentle nuzzling calmed Lightfoot's trembling.

Today Lightfoot had learned that the coyote was an enemy to fear. The little pronghorn would remember the lesson.

Lightfoot and Flagtail grew rapidly and by the time they were ten days old they were running with their mother. When they were three weeks old, most of their enemies could easily be left miles behind.

The young fawns loved to race, their long legs barely touching the ground. They ran with a graceful, effortless motion—their beautiful bodies soaring over log and brush.

Running was a game, and distance meant little. Sometimes the family traveled twenty or thirty miles a day for water. In a sudden burst of speed Lightfoot and Flagtail sprinted a mile a minute, but during a long chase they settled down to a normal run of forty miles an hour. Their enlarged windpipes made it easier for them to breathe, and so they could continue at this pace for many miles. They traveled without making a sound.

The only animal in the world who can run faster than the pronghorn is the cheetah.

About four weeks after they were born, the mother doe took her offspring back to join the herd. The youngsters were weaned and now they chewed the rich green grasses. They found other frisky playmates, and they raced together and, stiff-legged, leaped high into the air.

Lightfoot and Flagtail discovered that their relatives had "flags" to signal each other. When another pronghorn saw or scented danger, a patch of glistening white hair growing on his rump stood on end. When the bright sun shone on this patch, the brilliant flash of white could be seen by other pronghorn—sometimes as far

as three and four miles away. This was their warning signal of danger.

Lightfoot and Flagtail learned to depend on their speed and eyesight to protect themselves. On these plains they could easily see danger approaching and watch the movements of an enemy a mile away.

Because of this keen eyesight their actions were determined by what they saw rather than what they heard or smelled. Their bodies were well suited for traveling over the wide plains and rolling prairie land. The pronghorn was safe as long as the enemy was in sight, for then his speed and endurance protected him.

One sunny morning Lightfoot and Flagtail were contentedly chewing on the bitter stems of sagebrush when from a distant hill there came a sudden warning flash of white. Instantly the herd fled. Galloping together from all directions, the stampeding pronghorns began to string out in a single file, a doe taking the lead, while a buck brought up the rear.

They ran with the speed of the swift prairie wind. Up a knoll and over a gully they raced—and then to the top of a ridge. There they stood alert, outlined against the clear sky.

Curious, they turned to see what had caused the alarm, their great, dark eyes shining. This time it had only been the sudden sound of whirring wings—a flushed grouse had startled the herd into hasty flight.

Over the summer months ahead Lightfoot learned a great many lessons, but he had inherited from his ancestors one trait that often got him into trouble—his curiosity. He had to investigate every strange little animal that crossed his path.

One morning as Lightfoot was nosing among some puzzling mounds of dirt, a prairie dog scurried out of his hole. Lightfoot leaped backward. He heard a sharp bark. He looked down and saw a fat prairie dog standing on his hind legs.

The little prairie dog looked up at the pronghorn and angrily scolded him for sticking a foot in his front door.

Prairie dog towns are dangerous to an animal on the run—a slim hoof could easily slip into one of their holes.

Later a furry black and white animal lazily waddled past Lightfoot. For a moment Lightfoot stood and looked after him. He had to know more about this new odd-looking creature. He began to circle around it, slowly moving closer.

The animal stopped and turned his head to look at Lightfoot.

The pronghorn caught a whiff of a strange new smell. Puzzled, he turned his head to the side. Slowly he moved forward.

The little skunk stamped his front feet and, half-turning, raised his bushy striped tail.

Lightfoot did not heed the warning.

A strong-smelling liquid sprayed the pronghorn.

Lightfoot leaped backward. A terrible stench filled his eyes and his nostrils. He couldn't see. He couldn't breathe. Snorting,

Lightfoot rubbed his nose against the ground, trying to rid himself of the stifling odor. But it would be weeks before the strong smell would disappear.

The furry little skunk turned and slowly waddled away.

Today Lightfoot had learned that there was a *proper* distance to follow behind a skunk.

It was a hot August afternoon.

Lightfoot and Flagtail were browsing in the sagebrush. A snake coiled on a flat rock caught Lightfoot's attention. The encounter with the skunk had not cured Lightfoot of his curious nature—he walked toward the snake.

The snake wriggled off the rock and slithered across the ground. Lightfoot followed. There was a soft, rattling sound. Instinctively the pronghorn hesitated.

In an instant his mother was beside him. She bounded into the air. With all her weight on her sharp pointed toes, she struck down at the poisonous rattlesnake.

Again and again she leaped!

Soon the rattling noise stopped. The deadly snake lay still.

Over the summer months more and more wandering bands of pronghorn joined the herd and it grew very large. The herd had increased from about seventy animals to over four hundred.

In September Lightfoot and Flagtail had only small buttons for horns. But the full grown bucks' horns were twelve to eighteen inches long. They were set close to the eyes, curving back at the tips into a prong.

The bucks shed their hollow horns annually. Each year new horns grow inside the old ones, and as they grow they loosen the outworn sheaths which one day will fall away. The pronghorn is the only animal in the world with hollow, branched horns which are shed each year.

The big bucks use their horns to protect themselves and in their fencing battles with other males.

The season for mating began.

Lightfoot and Flagtail watched, puzzled, as the males prepared for their yearly battles.

It began in fun.

While grazing peacefully side by side, two bucks suddenly decided to spar. But after several playful thrusts, they tired of the game and soon stopped.

Often a clump of sagebrush became their target. With a sudden slashing of horns they attacked the bush. But the attack lasted only a minute or so, and they soon went back to their nibbling and cud-chewing.

As the days passed, the bucks' necks enlarged and strengthened until they were half again their usual size. Finally a day came when the big bucks pawed the ground, shook their heads and snorted their challenge in earnest.

The tournament was on.

Lightfoot watched. Excitement and tension settled over the herd as the dueling matches began. Standing three to four feet tall and weighing between 90 and 140 pounds, the bucks lowered their heads. With grace and skill, the males leaped high in the air, using their prongs as swords.

The "swordsmen" fenced skillfully—closing in, leaping apart, parrying and thrusting and waiting for a chance to jab.

Whenever a buck finally tired of the fight he turned and dashed away. He had to escape quickly or be badly hurt by the slashing horns.

Then the victor turned and claimed his mate. He had to fight other fierce battles to keep her and to acquire other mates, but he was willing and eager to do so.

One fall day Lightfoot heard sounds he had not heard before—the crack and whine of bullets. He had not connected sound with danger, but now a new and fearful enemy had come to pursue the pronghorn—man. The hunting season had begun. The handsome head of a pronghorn is a trophy prized by hunters.

Before the West was settled, French-Canadian explorers reported vast herds of pronghorn. Millions of these animals ranged from central Saskatchewan to central Mexico, and from western Iowa to the Rockies. Then pioneers and hunters came. They built towns, and plowed the land, and killed the pronghorn. The great herds were almost wiped out—by 1908 only 20,000 animals were left. Like the buffalo, the pronghorn were in danger of becoming extinct.

Just in time, laws were passed to protect the pronghorn, and today about 250,000 roam over the plains of Montana, Wyoming, and New Mexico, a small part of their original rangeland. Laws can protect the pronghorn from hunters, but the animals need miles and miles of wide open country to run and live in. Little by little the great stretches of land are disappearing.

During the hunting season the animals were constantly on the run. After weeks of terror and running, the Great Plains once more became still. The hunters had finally gone.

The nights became frosty and the prong-horns' fur coats grew thicker.

One morning, soft white snowflakes fell out of the gray sky. They tickled Lightfoot's nose and he and Flagtail leaped and played in the snow, not knowing that in a couple of months it would become a deadly trap.

Next to natural predators and man, snow is the greatest enemy of the pronghorn. It covers his food, and blizzard winds pile the snow into deep drifts, making it difficult for him to outrun his enemies.

On the plains Lightfoot found no shelter from the harsh winter winds. The days grew bitter cold, but Lightfoot's special coat of fur kept him from freezing. His coat was made of long, tightly packed hairs, full and deep. Each hair was hollow and filled with a pithlike sub-stance which acted as an insulation. The hairs kept the pronghorn's body heat from escaping, and even during the worst storm Lightfoot's fur coat protected him.

As the snow grew deeper, food became more and more scarce. The layer of fat that the pronghorn had developed over the summer months gradually disappeared. Now Lightfoot and Flagtail were always hungry.

Bushes that were not covered by snow had long ago been stripped clean by the hungry animals. Bark was peeled from the trunks of trees. Now even when Lightfoot stood on his hind legs and stretched his neck as high as he could, he was able to reach only a few mouthfuls of food.

The herd had to move further into the timber country to find food. This was dangerous, for it was hard to see an enemy among the trees and even harder to run from him.

Many animals starved during the cold winter.

Because it was difficult for them to run in the snowdrifts, many more were pulled down by hungry coyotes and cougars.

In the last week of March, a warm chinook wind blew down the slopes of the Rocky Mountains, melting the snows at last. Soon tender greens began to push through the dark earth.

Lightfoot and Flagtail were lucky—they had survived their first winter. They were thin and weak, but they were alive.

Early one morning, as the pronghorn were feeding on the new grass, there was a sudden

warning flash of white. The herd was off and running.

Three lean and hungry coyotes came down from the hills looking for food.

The herd of pronghorn ran in a great circle, easily outrunning the coyotes. But soon the cunning predators began to take turns chasing the herd. When one coyote became tired he rested while another took up the chase.

Lightfoot and Flagtail ran side by side. The hard winter began to tell on the animals and they ran more slowly. Lightfoot fell back, running a short way behind Flagtail.

Suddenly a streak of gray leaped out of the sagebrush straight at Flagtail's throat.

Lightfoot saw the coyote's snapping teeth. He leaped high.

Stiff-legged, his front hoofs drove downward. He struck the coyote's shoulder, and the shaggy killer rolled off balance. In seconds the two pronghorns bounded to one side and with a fresh burst of speed were safely away.

An exhausted old buck was not as lucky. He could not keep up. He fell back, running further and further behind the herd. He stumbled and the coyotes leaped in for the kill.

The rest of the herd ran free.

In May, the sagebrush and cactus burst into bloom. Songbirds returned and built new homes in the cottonwood trees while prairie chickens, pheasants, and grouse nested in the brush.

Once again the land was filled with the music and color of spring.

Soon the herd began to break up. The big bucks drifted away in twos and threes while the does went off by themselves to have their fawns.

Lightfoot and Flagtail stayed with the other yearlings.

From now on they were on their own.

Standing on a knoll, Lightfoot lifted his proud head and looked out over the wide, rolling plains, his dark eyes alert and watchful. Above and all about him were his enemies—coyote and cougar, eagle and bobcat. Man. Lightfoot always had to be on guard.

For here on the Great Plains run the pronghorn—the hunted.

ABOUT THE AUTHOR

All of Berniece Freschet's books are based on firsthand observation of nature, but this one has a special significance for her. Mrs. Freschet's father was a homesteader on the Powder River, and her two brothers were born in the log house he built there. Mrs. Freschet herself grew up in Montana, and has always enjoyed hiking and camping in the rugged northwest country. With her husband and five children she now lives in Lexington, Massachusetts.

ABOUT THE ARTIST

Robert Quackenbush was born in California and brought up in Arizona. He is a graduate of the Art Center College of Design in Los Angeles.

Mr. Quackenbush now lives in New York City, but he spends much of his time on painting excursions in Europe and the United States. He has illustrated more than fifty books for children and adults, for which he has received honors and citations from the Society of Illustrators and the American Institute of Graphic Arts. His work has been exhibited at leading museums throughout the country, including the Philadelphia Academy of Fine Arts and the Whitney Museum in New York City, and at his own gallery in New York, where he also teaches art.